IGNITE

How to **Fuel**
Your Soul's **Passion**
for **God**

KELLY PARKER

To: Devona

Kelly Parker

Col. 3:12

God bless you!

Ignite: How to Fuel Your Soul's Passion for God.
Copyright © 2018 by Kelly Parker. All rights reserved.

ISBN 978-164255137-2 (Softcover)

ISBN 978-164255138-9 (eBook)

Library of Congress Control Number: 2018903303

Editor: Bethany Clark
Cover design: Jesus Cordero
Back cover photo: Lavar Elliott Photography

Printed in the United States of America.

To my children, Gabrielle, Luvirt (Marcus), and Nia—think big, dream often, and follow God wherever He leads you.

To my husband, Luvirt—thank you for being the partner and friend I've needed, through good times and bad.

To my parents, Tyrone and Blondell—I am because of you. Thank you for your never-ending support.

To my people—those who pushed me to complete this project and encouraged me when I didn't think it was possible—you know who you are: I thank you.

CONTENTS

INTRODUCTION

You were not meant to be average.

God did not download into you a will, intellect, and emotions, things none of His other creations possess, for you to be mediocre. He did not give you a unique personality, gifts, and abilities for them to be halfheartedly, haphazardly used.

Just face it: from conception you have been exceptional! Your hair color, the inflection of your voice, your personality, and your disposition were all designed on purpose and will never be duplicated.

I hope these insightful facts give you a sense of dignity—pride, even. But can I tell you something? While I'm overjoyed to know God took such tender, loving care in creating me, I'm also a little afraid—afraid I'll just continue to get up every morning, mind my own business, and be moderately nice to people, yet the eternal impact of my life ends up marginal at best. In short, I'm afraid I'm living well below my God-given potential.

So I'm hoping and I'm praying that God will ignite something in me, something that cannot be easily extinguished or snuffed out—not a desire for things, notoriety, power, or prestige, but a passion for Him. And it's my hope and prayer that He will fan a flame deep within my soul to accomplish every single thing He's put me on this earth to do that no hardship, disappointment, or temptation could thwart.

These hopes and prayers are the reason for this book. This book is an invitation for you and me to reclaim a fire and passion for Jesus that we may have once known. Or it is a starting point for those of us who have heard about things like these but never experienced them ourselves. And for those of us in the midst of a season of great passion and fire for Jesus, this book offers practical tools and directives from the Word of God for how to stay there.

You and I have a window, a dash. It is the space between our birth date and death date. We have a limited opportunity to do the things God has called us to do. To maximize this opportunity, we've got to figure out how to set our souls ablaze for the things of God. That's what this book is all about.

For those who name the name of Jesus, this project is meant to serve as a wakeup call. It is a clarion call to wake up from our slumber, stand at attention, and be intentional about carrying out the mission and vision that God has for our lives: to bring Him glory and further His kingdom.

Wherever you find yourself today, welcome to *Ignite*.

CHAPTER 1

PREREQUISITES

As a college student, I had to create my schedule for each upcoming semester. I kept the requirements for my degree handy to make sure I was taking all the correct classes in order to finish. I realized that the classes needed to be taken in a certain order; they built on one another. In fact, the university wouldn't even allow students to register for higher level classes without getting passing grades in their more basic classes, called prerequisites.

Many of us long to live with a burning fire and passion for God, to walk fully in our purpose and have clarity and direction for our lives, but we have yet to fulfill the prerequisites. There's one prerequisite I'd like to focus on in particular. If you're avoiding this class or you've signed up but continue to fail every test the Teacher gives, then the burning passion for God you're looking for will continue to elude you.

This class is called Surrender.

The heart that is completely yielded to God is the heart that is aimed, ready, and positioned to receive everything He has in store.

A Combustible Heart

Heathcliff Huxtable, Bill Cosby's iconic character on the '80s and '90s sitcom *The Cosby Show*, enjoyed a successful track career in his younger days. He ran with so much power and vigor that he earned the nickname "Combustible Huxtable."

God wants to make you combustible. When you come into contact with Him, He wants it to spark a flame that infiltrates your whole being. Do you know what it's going to take for you to be combustible? Can you guess what the prerequisite for this kind of life might be?

Surrender.

A totally surrendered heart is combustible. It's an environment ripe and ready for God to come in and work.

Many moons ago, twelve unassuming, unsuspecting men learned about surrender when their yielded, combustible hearts turned the world on its head. They impacted every sector of the world they lived in. They didn't have fancy clothes, hefty bank accounts, or lavish lifestyles. Their impact did not come from power, prestige, or political notoriety. It came from the inferno that ensued when they encountered God Himself and realized they'd been entrusted with the very thing that would change the world.

These souls, better known as the twelve disciples, served God in extreme danger and trial, lacking many of the modern comforts and conveniences you and I have today. It would seem to me that living in our day and age with abundant spiritual resources, our resolve to surrender to the Lord would be even stronger than that of those early Christians. With open access to the Bible and a plethora of Bible studies, books, sermons, and other resources at our fingertips, some might say we have the superior circumstance.

So why then do we have so many churches with so little life change? And building funds but no breakthroughs? Church programs but no power?

I believe it is because we have treated surrender, a critical, foundational prerequisite for a powerful Christian life, as a completely optional undertaking.

In the book of Acts, we see that when the disciples' surrendered hearts encountered the risen Savior, fear turned to faith. Their timidity turned to vehement conviction. Lack of life purpose turned to clarity. All of a sudden, they had boldness, courage, and steadfastness that were not and could not be shaken by the gravest dangers or the most difficult life circumstances.

I believe you and I have the power to do the same thing if we'd resolve here and now to avoid two very common surrender-sabotaging pitfalls:

1. Endless Options

As first-century Christians, the disciples faced harsh persecution and were treated as outcasts. They clung to each other and to God. That was it. There were no other options. The situation was too dire.

And herein lies one of the difficulties of modern Western culture: we are inundated with options. The Word of God represents just one among many viewpoints we think we can pick and choose to appropriate in our lives. More often than not, we have a list a mile long of all the different avenues we will explore, searching for truth and direction for our lives. We call our friends, our co-workers, our significant others, our parents, our sisters, our brothers. We explore our own reasoning. Then it's social media. After that, we do a thorough investigation into what pop psychology has to offer. Once we've exhausted all those options, we mosey on over to the Word of God to see what it has to say. But if the Word doesn't jive with other, more palatable options we've discovered, then we're quick to cast it aside, confident that our intellectual prowess is superior to God's.

We have too many options. The surrendered heart navigates as quickly as possible to the voice and direction of the Lord, forsaking all others, exchanging its own agenda for God's. It forsakes plans B, C, and D for plan A alone.

In John 6, after Jesus had shared some teachings that were difficult to understand, many of His disciples turned back and decided not to walk with Him. In response, Jesus turned to the twelve, asking them if they intended to turn back as well. Peter said, "Lord, to whom shall we go? You have the words to eternal life, and we have believed, and have come to know, that you are the Holy One of God" (John 6:68–69). The twelve disciples understood that no one else could satisfy the deepest longing of their souls: to have connection with the Father. They had no interest in entertaining any other alternatives.

> If you have not yet tired of your options, then your heart is not yet ready to receive God's best.

If you have not yet tired of your options, then your heart is not yet ready to receive God's best.

Are you convinced that God's way is best? Have you purposed in your mind that you will trust He has the words to eternal life?

2. The Pursuit of Comfort

Added to our tendency to weigh all viable options, no matter how ungodly they may be, is our culture's obsession with comfort. Even in the church, we are sometimes focused on a quick-fix, path-of-least-resistance approach to life. Our insatiable desire and our demand for comfort circumvent our efforts to gain the traction in our walk with God we're looking for. We think, *Will it make me happy? Is this something I feel like doing? What's the easiest thing for me to do?*

If this is the kind of thinking that drives your spiritual life above what God has already said, then you will find that the passion and fervor you're looking for will continue to slip through your fingers.

A fixation on comfort was foreign to the New Testament church. More important than pleasure and convenience was the spreading of the gospel, no matter the cost. In the book of Acts, we see the apostle Paul, for instance, relentlessly traveling from place to place with the good news of Jesus, despite danger and hardship. The early believers were beaten, arrested, and even thrown in jail, yet they endured their circumstances with joy, knowing that their plight served a much bigger purpose (see Acts 5:41; 13:51–52).

Yielding to God

Only those who are ready to surrender wholeheartedly and completely to God's ways will experience the fire and intensity their souls seek. At its core, your level of passion for God is related to the depth of your level of surrender to Him.

To surrender means to yield. When your ideas and God's ideas bump heads, surrender is an emphatic, willful deferral to God's way instead of yours. Surrender is what Jesus did in the Garden of Gethsemane, when He was confronted with the reality of His impending death. At the height of His

> Only those who are ready to surrender wholeheartedly and completely to God's ways will experience the fire and intensity their souls seek.

anguish and despair, He said to the Father, "Not as I will, but as you will" (Matthew 26:39). Surrender is what Mary displayed after finding out that she, an unwed young girl, would give birth to the Savior of the world, when she said to the angel, "Behold, I am the servant of the Lord; let it be to me according to your word" (Luke 1:38). Though she didn't fully understand what was going on, and likely would have preferred other circumstances, she made a decision to follow God's path for her life.

Are you ready for that? Is that something that you truly want? When you say "right" and God says "left," are you willing to backtrack, inconvenient and counterintuitive as it may be, to obey His way instead of yours?

This is not the time to give the textbook yes answer, lest you find yourself grappling with these same issues five, ten, or fifteen years from now because you didn't want to be honest with yourself. If you sense some areas in your life where your answer is, in effect, "No, God, I actually think I know better than You in this area. I'm not quite sure if I can trust You with this," then I'm going to suggest something. Lock yourself in a room. Or go outside. Depending on your living situation and life stage, this might be easier said than done, but wherever you go, find some uninterrupted time alone. And say the words out loud—what's really on your heart. Don't say what you're supposed to say. Say what's really there. Express the "I'm not sure"s and the "I don't believe"s. Speak honestly about the reservations you have. Ask Him to help you. Ask Him to guide you.

I'm not kidding, you guys. You can do all the due diligence in the world, you can read the rest of this book, you can go to all the Bible studies and all the Christian conferences, and you can like all the inspirational quotes on social media, but if you've made up your mind that you'd rather have your options and your comfort than surrender your whole self to the will of the Lord, then it's just not going to work. No fire is going to spark because you're not combustible enough. The conditions of your heart won't allow the fire to catch.

But I have to warn you: surrender is not a one-and-done kind of thing. It's a lifestyle of frequenting your locked room to pour your heart out before the Lord. Some of us have been walking with the Lord for a while, and if we're honest, there are some corners and pockets we still haven't surrendered, and we've settled for a lackluster Christian experience because of it. So go to God and say what you need to say. Or write it down if you have to. Whatever comes bubbling up, let it out. If it's tears, let them flow. If it's anger, hurt, or disappointment, empty it out so that God can fill you anew. The trajectory of your Christian life depends on it.

CHAPTER 2

JUST SAY YES

I first became serious about my walk with Jesus as a college student at Kent State University.

As I ventured off to college in the fall of 2001, I was excited to finally get away from home and explore the world on my terms. I quickly joined a campus Bible study group. Growing up immersed in church culture, this seemed like the right thing to do. I figured I could go to the hour-long meeting each week and then be on my merry way. I had no idea that what I would encounter there would change the path of the rest of my life.

The first thing I noticed was that the young people in this group were not just studying the Bible; they were living it. Their lives contrasted so much with many of the examples I had seen earlier in life, in which God was a high priority on Sunday but virtually nonexistent on the other days of the week.

At first, it was all too fanatical for my taste. I didn't understand why these people wanted to get together all the time. Wasn't the weekly meeting enough?

I was also turned off by things they considered normal, like studying their Bibles together in public places—where people could see. Weird.

As weird as it was, it was also very attractive. Because they were seeking to live out their faith, these students had a sense of genuineness in their walk with God—something I didn't have.

Before I knew it, the fanatic, the zealot, the crazy girl trying to talk total strangers into spending their evening studying the Bible was . . . me. A fire and a passion for Jesus had been lit and I didn't care who knew it.

My Bible-study friends and I traveled to Washington, DC, for the Impact Movement National Conference. In addition to hearing great preaching and sitting in on amazing breakout sessions, we were tasked to hop on a school bus and take the gospel of Jesus Christ to the streets. With boxes of love (which had non-perishable food items) and tracts in hand, we were dropped off in a nearby residential area and challenged to knock on some doors and share the good news of Jesus.

For our first stop, three of my friends and I ended up at the home of Aaron Lightfoot. When he answered the door, we cheerfully held out a box of love, along with the offer to tell him more about Jesus with our very handy *Four Spiritual Laws* booklet. Looking us over, he said, "Do you see that Benz back there?" He pointed to the car parked behind us on the street. We nodded. "That's mine. Give that box to someone who needs it." And politely as one can, he shut the door in our faces.

It took a couple of minutes to wipe the dazed, deer-in-headlights looks from our faces, but undaunted, we marched on.

The next house we approached had a young man about my age sitting on the front steps. I walked up to him and asked him if I could go through the gospel tract I had with me. To my surprise, he said yes. I found out his name was Loomis. He and I went through the booklet page by page, and when we got to the end, I asked him what he wanted to do next. He said he wanted to invite Jesus into his heart. I didn't know all the right words to say, but I prayed for Loomis that day. I told the Lord that Loomis needed Him and that he wanted to accept Jesus into his heart.

I think about Loomis from time to time. I wonder if he's standing strong in the faith. I wonder how he's navigating the ups and downs, the spiritual highs and lows we all face. I wonder if he feels the same way I do: that living out this Christianity thing is the fight of your life.

In the midst of my conversation with Loomis, several other people came out of the house. My friends struck up conversations with them, sharing the good news of the gospel. And next thing you know, we were all gathered in a circle holding hands and praying, right there in the front yard.

It all started with a yes. Yes to the potential for being rejected or looking foolish or weird. Yes to being uncomfortable. Yes to the unknown. And yes to the opportunity to see, witness, and experience things that only God can do.

But time has passed between then and now. I've settled a bit into the rhythm of daily schedules and responsibilities. And I have to admit that my willingness to say yes to discomfort and inconvenience at Jesus' request has cooled a bit. I don't know if I'd be as quick today to walk around an unfamiliar neighborhood and approach complete strangers as I was back then. There seems to be more of a sense in which I just want to get by and blend into the crowd.

As we discussed, surrender is a key component to living out your Christian faith with vigor and passion. One way to measure your level of surrender is by how long it takes you to say yes when you feel God prompting you to act. This statement will help you to remember this principle:

If your yeses are slow, your surrender is low.

The longer it takes you to act in obedience to God, the more likely it is that there are some areas of resistance in your heart that need to be surrendered to the Lord.

> If your yeses are slow, your surrender is low.

So often we allow our feelings to impact our decision to say yes to God. We figure we will obey God when we feel like it, when we're ready. But when we think like this, we have the steps all out of order. The yes that comes from a surrendered heart must already be there in order for the fire to be sparked in the first place. It's what makes us combustible.

> Consistent passion for God is not based on feelings alone. Instead, it must be grounded in a decision to say yes to Him no matter what.

Consistent passion for God is not based on feelings alone. Instead, it must be grounded in a decision to say yes to Him no matter what.

Spiritual Paralysis

Scripture uses an interesting analogy to depict believers' relationship to Christ. The Bible says that He is the head and we are the body. We get our marching orders from the head (Christ) and then we, the body, are expected to do the work. We are tasked to be His hands and feet, carrying out the mission that God conceived in eternity past and jumpstarted with Jesus' earthly ministry.

But it seems that we sometimes suffer from spiritual paralysis. God is sending out orders to the body, but there is an internal malfunction in the form of lack of surrender and an unwillingness to say yes to His direction, so the orders don't get carried out. He tells the foot to go and share the love of Jesus with a friend. But the foot is so entangled in fear and bitterness that it can't bring itself to obey the order. He tells the hand to serve people with whom he or she might not normally associate. But the hand has allowed the decaying effects of prolonged self-centeredness to prevent it from functioning properly. In effect, the body grows desensitized to the directives of the head.

When I was in eighth and ninth grade, I (briefly!) ran track. My event was the 4x400 relay. Our coach adamantly told us on more than one occasion, "If you let that baton hit the ground, just keep running 'til you reach your house." Why? Because in relay, the baton hitting the ground means game over. It means you couldn't successfully transition from one runner to the next and, for that, you're disqualified.

Jesus has passed you the baton. Are you running with it by saying yes to Him, or are you letting it drop to the ground by saying no?

Ephesians 2:10 says, "For we are his workmanship, created in Christ Jesus for good works, which God prepared beforehand, that we should walk in them." This verse speaks to the work God has called us to do by which we will change the world.

The only trouble is, we figure we have all the time in the world to get things figured out: "Later for that. Next year I'll get more into my spiritual life." Don't minimize the blessings and opportunities you are forfeiting because you are slow to get on board and align your life with God's directives.

In healing a man blind from birth, Jesus makes an interesting statement about the works of God. He tells His disciples, "We must work the works of him who sent me while it is day; night is coming, when no one can work" (John 9:4). "Day" represented Jesus' time on Earth, the time He'd

> "Don't minimize the blessings and opportunities you are forfeiting because you are slow to get on board and align your life with God's directives."

been given to complete His Father's mission. Jesus pointed out that He was aware that "night" was coming, when He would leave this earth and could work the works of the Father no longer.

Jesus, now dwelling in a human body, was acutely aware of the fleeting nature of the time allotted to Him to complete His earthly mission. He knew that He only had a certain number of years, days, hours, and minutes to complete the mission, or to "work the works" of the Father. His window of opportunity wouldn't last forever.

Do we live with the same awareness Jesus had about the limited time we have to complete our part in the Father's mission?

There's this prevailing thinking that we have all these stored-up moments in the future to do the things we know we should do and become the people God has called us to be. It's as if we believe we can afford to delay our efforts to please God for some time and pick them back up at a later, more convenient date. But this is not the model Jesus has put forth in Scripture.

In the midst of warning against boastful business practices, the writer of James points out that in all our planning and projecting, we should not forget that we "do not know what tomorrow will bring." He continues, "What is your life? For you are a mist that appears for a little time and then vanishes" (James 4:14).

At the end of the day, we have no idea what tomorrow will bring or how many more tomorrows we will have. So choosing to delay our fulfillment of God's assignments for us is a pretty big gamble.

So what should we do?

Do it now.

Whatever you sense God impressing upon you to do, do it now.

Is He telling you to take steps to start a business or ministry? Do it now.

Is He nudging you to put away thoughts, habits, and actions that don't line up with His Word? Do it now.

Is He prodding you to get out of your comfort zone and use your gifts and talents to serve others? Do it now.

Without a doubt, we must thoroughly sift everything we do in prayer and listen to wise counsel to protect ourselves from jumping headfirst into something God hasn't even called us to. But don't use your fear of getting it wrong as a cop-out. Figure out what God wants you to do and get busy. Just take the first step. After all, you might not have as much time as you think you do.

Now that we've laid the groundwork for creating a fire in our hearts for God through surrender and obedience, we're ready to dive into some very specific and practical ways to fuel that passion within our souls. After each chapter, you'll find space for Spark Notes. These are key takeaways, reflections and action steps you feel God impressing on your heart based on what you've read. Feel free to use the space provided to record memory verses, prayers, lists, or anything else that will inspire you to think deeply and apply the concepts in this book.

Brace yourself. This is going to be a wild ride.

Part 1
DESTROY

CHAPTER 3

UP IN FLAMES

In 2016, a fire broke out at the Institute of Criminology in Brussels, Belgium. It took dozens of firefighters to squelch the blaze. No casualties were reported, but witnesses were alarmed at the sound of the ensuing explosion.

In reviewing the scene, officials quickly determined that this inferno was no accident. Destroyed in the fire was a laboratory used to analyze DNA samples collected at crime scenes—the same DNA historically used to link and convict people to crimes. The perpetrators set the fire to destroy valuable evidence.

Fire destroys. It has the unique ability to annihilate and dismember anything in its path. As we surrender our whole hearts to God in search of the deep-seated passion and fire our soul seeks, we will find along the way that there are a few things that need to be destroyed.

When we say yes to a relationship with God through Jesus Christ, God invites us on a journey with Him. It's an unpredictable journey full of twists and turns, ups and downs. Considering that the length of this journey is lifelong, God allows us to take along some items for the trip, a spiritual knapsack, if you will. He knows we're new to the terrain, so at first, He lets us take along whatever we like.

To accompany your newfound declaration of faith, you have likely chosen things like love, patience, and compassion for the journey. But inevitably, things like selfishness, anger, jealousy, pride, and deceit have found their way into your knapsack as well.

As you and your Lord journey together, with your permission, of course, God begins to explore the items you've packed for the trip. When He finds items consistent with His nature, it pleases Him, and He shows you how to experience those things in even greater measure. If He sees love in your bag, He commends you for it because He is love. When He sees compassion in your bag, His heart is made happy because your heart mirrors His.

But from time to time, after sundown, when you make camp for the night and you sit near the campfire to warm yourself, God stumbles across something in your bag that troubles Him because He knows it will hinder you on your journey. And He turns to you and tells you this is the part in the journey where you must let it go—all your crutches and hidden sins, the bad habits you picked up as a child that you just can't seem to break, the bad attitude, the lust, the envy, the pride. He tells you it's time to throw it into the fire and destroy it for good.

It is at this moment that we have a critical choice to make. Will we hold our knapsack tightly to our chest, insisting that our fear, sin, and limiting thought patterns are here to stay? Or will we, with heart racing and hands trembling, obey the voice of the Lord and forsake everything we have known so that we can give birth to the purpose and destiny God has had for us all along?

Can I be honest? At times I've gotten this right and willingly obeyed. But sometimes, I get it wrong. Sometimes, I'm just way too comfortable in my typical way of doing things to acknowledge the fact that by bypassing God's best for me, I'm actually sabotaging myself.

When your surrendered heart encounters the living God and that fire starts to spark, everything in you not consistent with His nature will get destroyed. Your willingness to cooperate in this process will determine the intensity of the flames. This process doesn't happen all at once or in a day. On the contrary, it is a lifelong journey that describes the experience of every true believer.

God wants to destroy everything about you that isn't consistent with His nature because He knows it won't serve you well on your journey to fulfill your destiny.

Sounds painful, doesn't it?

It is.

But aren't you thankful that it's not the kind of pain that doesn't amount to anything—that obnoxious, pointless pain, like stubbing your toe on the edge of the bed? No, it's the kind of pain that has a purpose, that accomplishes a desired outcome. It's much like going through the aches and pains of childbirth to bring about new life.

> God wants to destroy everything about you that isn't consistent with His nature.

Labor Pains

On a snowy day in January 2012, I woke up knowing that today would be the day. After nine months of morning sickness, backaches, and swollen feet, it was time for me to give birth to our third and final (emphasis on final) child. I told my husband that I felt like this would be the day, and he politely nodded, as if to say, "Yes, dear, that's very nice," as if he was a little skeptical—or unmoved, even—about my declaration. I was a little confused about his lack of emotional response, but he's not really an over-the-top, dramatic kind of guy, so I brushed it off. Besides, there was much work to be done. I didn't have time to dwell on such things.

I waddled up the steps to pack an overnight bag (why hadn't I done that already?) for my other two kids. But with every move I made, the pain seemed to double, triple, and quadruple in magnitude until all I could do was lie on the floor with each contraction, waiting for the pain to subside.

I announced to my husband that we couldn't wait any longer and we needed to get to the hospital right away, to which he responded, while washing dishes and packing up garbage to take outside, that I should lie down. It was as if he believed living through the prolonged labors of our other two children gave him some expertise on this particular day. Clearly, it did not.

Once my mother finally arrived to pick up our two-year-old and four-year-old, we headed out.

I got myself positioned in the car and finally started to feel relieved that we were making some progress. So when I made the discovery that there was no gas in said car, I was a little . . . perturbed. Now, you've got to understand something. I've never been one of those adorable pregnant people who can fit in their regular clothes until the last two days of their pregnancy and frolic about in four-inch high heels while doing it. Nope, not me. I was a planet. Couple that with the fact that this planet was in a whole lot of pain. Sure, we had another car with gas sitting in the driveway, but when I got into that car, I didn't want to move. I didn't even feel like I could.

Have you ever been in so much pain that you're convinced it can't get any worse and then that's the exact moment it gets so much worse? Yeah, that's what happened to me that day. We were flying down the freeway when I heard myself say, "My water just broke! Call 9-1-1!"

Although we were extremely close to the hospital, we just couldn't make it. I gave birth to Nia Grace Parker in my car on the side of the road in some stranger's yard, right off the freeway, with the help of a disoriented husband and an ambulance crew that arrived just in time.

The second she was born, my shrieks of "Somebody help me! Somebody help me!" were replaced with calm. A peace. An inner quietness. So much so that one of the ambulance workers looked up at me and said, "Ma'am, are you okay? You're so quiet."

I looked back at him and said, "I'm fine. You don't understand how good I feel."

Relief. Peace. Calm. This is what we have to look forward to on the other side of the pain that will come as God destroys some things out of our lives. It's pain that serves a deep and profound purpose.

Had I not gone through the pain, as dramatic and terrifying as the whole ordeal was, I wouldn't have given birth to my child. And so it is with you. Could it be that you have not yet given birth to the dreams, visions, and destiny God has for you because you don't want to go through the pain of letting go of things you've held near and dear for far too long?

So much of what we pray for is on the other side of our pain. So much of what we seek is birthed out of the process of God dismantling anything and everything in our lives that doesn't line up with His Word. When we navigate this process, we will find things like...

- Fullness of joy
- Freedom
- Transformation
- Breakthrough
- Deliverance
- Peace of mind
- Contentment
- Clarity
- Purpose
- Direction

One thing I love about God is that He thinks of everything. Thank God He does not require you to change habits and thought patterns you've clung to for years and then leave you to work it all out yourself! Knowing that we would not be able to accomplish this process of transforming into something new and like Him on our own, He left us with a guide who will direct us always. John 16:13 says, "When the Spirit of truth comes, he will guide you into all the truth, for he will not speak on his own authority, but whatever he hears he will speak, and he will declare to you the things that are to come." If you are a true believer in Jesus Christ, God has blessed you with the Holy Spirit to walk with you, step by step and day by day, on this journey. You don't have to go it alone.

That's God's desire for you: that each second, day, and hour you walk lockstep with Him, through His Spirit. But the more you try to hold on to things He's asked you to destroy, you'll find that you're not walking step by step, hand in hand with God. There will be distance between the two of you. It will be harder for you to perceive and understand His direction. And without Him close by, your spiritual passion will begin to fizzle. There's no fire for God without close connection with God Himself.

> "There's no fire for God without close connection with God Himself."

SPARK NOTES

CHAPTER 4

COUNTING WRONG

In Luke 14, Jesus described the cost of having relationship with Him. He said, "If anyone comes to me and does not hate his own father and mother and wife and children and brothers and sisters, yes, and even his own life, he cannot be my disciple. Whoever does not bear his own cross and come after me cannot be my disciple." He went on to say, "For which of you, desiring to build a tower, does not first sit down and count the cost, whether he has enough to complete it?" (Luke 14:26, 28).

Jesus warned people against making rash decisions in following Him. He encouraged them to "count the cost," or carefully consider the level of commitment and allegiance such a decision will require. Indeed, there is a price to be paid in following Jesus, both an initial cost in our first decision to follow Him as well as the costs on a day-to-day level.

So some of us have dug into our spiritual pockets, carefully doled out the amount of commitment we're able to comfortably offer God (without any pain or discomfort, that is), and figured we could keep the change. We figure, we counted the cost, we're paying what we can afford, so let's just leave it at that.

But have you considered the cost of *not* following Jesus? Obedience to Jesus is certainly quite expensive, but you didn't think disobedience was free, did you?

Everything costs, even our disobedience. So we don't get to opt out of Jesus' invitation to follow Him wholeheartedly and then keep the change. We actually give the difference to other things. And we get things like discontentment, discord, lack of peace, confusion, and intense discouragement in return.

Are you racking your brain trying to figure out why you're not experiencing more victory and intimacy in your spiritual life? Could it be that it's the price you're paying for your lack of obedience?

I don't mean to suggest that experiencing hardships or dry spiritual seasons is always evidence of a life of disobedience. Certainly, it is not. My point is that it is nearly impossible to experience consistent spiritual victory apart from a willingness to rid yourself of anything in your life that's not like Jesus.

The dividends we pay in obedience are an investment. We will reap a plentiful reward later. Our disobedience, on the other hand, will always result in some level of loss, and at the height of that loss are distance and disconnectedness in our relationship with God.

The principle is pretty simple: those who have a passion for Jesus are in the practice of destroying everything that comes between the two of them, no matter how uncomfortable or inconvenient that process might be.

Let me put it another way: destroy sin or it will destroy you. Why not commit to go through the process so that God can bring

about something beautiful in
your life and accomplish His
purposes through you?

> "Destroy sin or it will
> destroy you."

Weakened Soldiers

One of the biggest costs we pay for not destroying sin is
diminished effectiveness in spiritual battle. Like it or not, every
believer in Jesus Christ is in battle with Satan and his band,
including the "spiritual forces of evil in the heavenly places"
(Ephesians 6:12). To stand against the enemy's schemes, one of
the things we're instructed to do is to put on the breastplate of
righteousness (see Ephesians 6:14). The breastplate was a metal
shield that protected a soldier's most vital organ: his heart. In
other words, righteous living is a defensive weapon against the
enemy because it protects the very core of our being.

Pastor and Bible teacher John MacArthur says, "If you
go out to battle with a hole in the breastplate of personal
righteousness, Satan will jab you every time."[1] If you aren't
open to obeying the Lord's instructions about what needs to be
destroyed in your life, then you're leaving yourself wide open
to the enemy's attacks.

What are some of the things God might want you to
destroy? The possibilities are numerous, but let me give you a
few places to start.

Self-Centered Mentality

Growing up as an only child, it was a rather sobering, earth-
shattering moment when I discovered the truth that life isn't
always all about me. To be perfectly honest, I'm still learning
this lesson. All other things being equal, I advocate for every

circumstance to line up to my liking, with my preferences, my comfort, and my thoughts and opinions in mind.

My, my, my.

I don't think I'm the only one. We're entrenched in a society that reinforces the mindset of me first, you second.

This me-first mentality seems to be foreign to the early church. Acts 2:44–45 says, "And all who believed were together and had all things in common. And they were selling their possessions and belongings and distributing the proceeds to all, as any had need."

These believers were known for voluntarily giving of what they had to make sure others had what they needed. They didn't give out of compulsion or command but out of a genuine love for one another, even if it was a personal inconvenience for them.

Many times our passion for God is weak because we're so absorbed with our own wants and desires that we haven't stopped to ponder how God might want to use us in the life of someone else. The apostle Paul echoes these sentiments in Philippians 2:3–4 when he wrote, "Do nothing from selfish ambition or conceit, but in humility count others more significant than yourselves. Let each of you look not only to his own interests, but also to the interests of others."

It's interesting to note that we're not instructed to stop looking out for our own interests. Instead, the caution here is that we don't become so consumed with our own interests that we forget to have the same intensity of concern for the needs of others.

A self-absorbed life is often a spiritually passionless

> A self-absorbed life is often a spiritually passionless life.

life. If you're looking for a vibrant, on-fire experience with Jesus, extend your focus to include the well-being of others.

Front and Center for All to See

The life we live outwardly should line up with the Word of God. All too often, it's hard to tell by lifestyle choices alone the Christians from the non-Christians. In David Kinnaman and Gabe Lyons's book *unChristian: What a New Generation Really Thinks About Christianity . . . and Why It Matters,* church outsiders from the ages of 16 to 24 were surveyed. Only 15 percent of respondents said they could see any lifestyle difference between themselves and people they knew who they believed to be Christians.[2] To put it another way, the vast majority of people they knew who were Christians lived just like they did.

We live in a day and age where we think all God wants to do is give us an encouraging, inspirational word on Sunday, while we do whatever we feel like doing Monday through Saturday. But before you believe the hype, read the fine print. This double-life theology is like a strong wind that will quickly smother the flames of zeal and passion in your walk with God.

Is there an aspect of your lifestyle that needs to be destroyed and rebuilt so that it can be replaced with something far better? Maybe it's your sexuality, your work ethic, or the kinds of entertainment you enjoy. Whatever it might be, resolve to submit that area of your life so that God can lead you toward spiritual victory.

Creeping Under the Surface

For some us, by the grace of God, we've nipped most of the big stuff in the bud. You quit the drinking and partying and the sex and the drugs and whatever your particular sin of choice might have been back in the day. So you feel your lifestyle matches up just fine with the Word of God. Or maybe you've never participated in any of those types of things, so when these sorts of conversations come up, you pat yourself on the back for having yourself so together. In fact, maybe you've been reading this chapter contemplating what it is that God wants to destroy in you, but you can't seem to come up with anything.

My friend, you might be in the most trouble of all.

Until the day you and I see Jesus, we all have something somewhere in our lives that God wants us to toss out so that it can be replaced with something more like Him. And if you're unaware of the specific work God wants to do in a particular season of your life to conform you into His image, then it's possible you and Jesus aren't as close as you might think.

Passion for Jesus is fueled by awareness of our need for Jesus.

Can I say that again?

Passion for Jesus is fueled by awareness of our need for Jesus.

When we think we've got it all together or we're not really that bad off, we create distance between God and ourselves, even as believers. Having an ongoing, acute knowledge of our weak points keeps us highly aware of our need for God's help. It keeps Him relevant to us. It keeps the fire burning.

> **"Passion for Jesus is fueled by awareness of our need for Jesus."**

The sad reality is that many of us are out of touch with the work God wants to do in us because we don't want to hear the truth about the dark areas of our hearts. Such things are inconsistent with the image of ourselves we've created in our heads: the church-going, pious, angelic parishioners we wish we were. We don't want to own up to the work that still needs to be done in our hearts.

And when you've stopped doing the big stuff, the "little" stuff is rather easy to avoid, because most of the work that's still left to do in your heart is inward; it's unseen. At this stage in the game, it's easy to fool the masses into thinking you've got your act together, but behind closed doors, the intimacy and fire with Jesus you say you've always wanted has grown cold.

In short, we end up keeping God at arm's length with our self-righteousness and pride and are left with a mediocre, lackluster experience with God because of it.

> The sacrifices of God are a broken spirit; a broken and contrite heart, O God, you will not despise. (Psalm 51:17)

> Pride goes before destruction, and a haughty spirit before a fall. (Proverbs 16:18)

What are some of these creepy-crawlers that lie beneath the surface, undetected by most people around us, but need to be destroyed nonetheless? This list will get you started, but I'm sure you can think of even more:

- Bitterness
- Jealousy
- Envy
- Pride
- Unforgiveness

- Arrogance
- Haughtiness
- Selfishness

Did you notice what many of these things have in common? They are relational concepts. They have to do with how we treat one another. Too often we focus on getting rid of the outward "big" sins but haven't forsaken these below-the-surface creepy-crawlers. So even in the church, we have a whole bunch of outwardly holy people who can't get along because they refuse to apply what the Bible says to the unseen places of their heart. When interpersonal tensions arise, we're slow to acknowledge that we have some growing and destroying to do. It's always the other person who's at fault.

And then, drenched in our pride and self-righteousness, we wonder why our experience with God seems to be lacking.

SPARK NOTES

CHAPTER 5

WELL WORTH THE EFFORT

I want to repeat my earlier question but this time emphasize the word "specific."

Can you pinpoint *specific* areas in your life in which God wants to do a destroying work to draw you to Himself?

I'm not talking about the generic "I know I'm a sinner." I'm not even talking about blanket statements such as "I've got a problem with pride." Be specific. How does this issue play out in your life? What specifically are you doing, thinking, and saying that's due to this issue? What are you missing out on due to it? How has it affected those around you? Do you see it as a problem? Why haven't you given it up yet?

People with a deep love and palpable passion for God tend to be very aware of where God is working in their lives and is trying to change them. It's not always about what they used to do with these people. It's also about what He's doing right now and what areas He currently wants to develop.

You might not consider your answer to this question to be particularly grand or a big deal, but it is obedience to God in the smallest of things that opens the door for us to see and experience Him in even bigger ways.

Keep Up the Good Work

I can remember working full-time in corporate America with three little ones at home and lamenting about the lack of time I had to keep my house in order. So when I left my job to enter a season of stay-at-home motherhood, I couldn't wait to give my

> " Obedience to God in the smallest of things opens the door to see and experience Him in even bigger ways. "

bathrooms a good deep clean. It's weird but true. When I was finished, I stood back for a moment, admiring the shining porcelain and glimmering stainless steel.

But much to my dismay, within a few days (or was it hours?), it looked like I'd never lifted a finger to clean a thing! So I had to get out the Pine Sol and the Clorox and the Comet all over again and get to work.

It was then that I was reminded of something I'd known all along: the upkeep of this house takes continual work.

The same is true for your spiritual house. You don't come to Jesus one day, invite Him into your life, and then skip off on your own for the rest of your life. That's not the way He designed it. You can go that route if you want to, but soon you'll realize that your house is a mess! Instead, you have to check in with Him continually to keep things on track, putting in the effort it takes to keep things in working order.

This side of eternity, you will never outgrow your need to engage with Jesus on a continual basis to see where He is inviting you to change and grow. In Luke 9:23, Jesus said, "If anyone would come after me, let him deny himself and take up his cross daily and follow me." The imagery of taking up your cross in crucifixion is jarring imagery to depict what it means to follow Jesus. The idea is that Jesus requires that we embrace what He wants for us, no matter the cost—continually. Not once a year. Not occasionally. Not every now and then, but on an ongoing basis.

I think one of the most interesting people we meet in the Bible is Peter. While Paul seems to be a Super Saint of sorts, nearly always making the right choices and saying the right things once he makes the decision to follow Jesus, Peter is more impulsive and gregarious—even controversial at times. After walking and talking with Jesus so intimately for years, Peter denied that he ever even knew Jesus after His arrest—not once, not even twice, but *three* times. Then, after becoming a pillar of the church who spoke so boldly in the book of Acts, Peter was caught in hypocrisy in Galatians 2, so much so that he led other believers astray.

What I love is how God is able to use both the Pauls and the Peters of the world to advance His agenda. As much as we might like to, no one gets this thing right 100 percent of the time. But despite our flaws and shortcomings, God can use anyone or anything as a catalyst to do His will.

Peter's life is also a reminder that you can't build your walk with Jesus on past victories or past failures. Past spiritual victories do not necessarily guarantee future ones. We must stay in a constant, continual state of connection with the Father to experience success.

How much effort do you put into staying in regular connection with the Father, allowing Him to pinpoint the exact areas where He wants to transform you?

If your answer to that question isn't what you'd like it to be, don't despair! God is ready and willing to nurture, teach, shepherd, comfort, and guide you right where He wants you, but only if you'll let Him do the work.

> We must stay in a constant, continual state of connection with the Father to experience success.

A Wise Investment

If you've ever invested in mutual funds, you know it's possible to look up the performance of each stock and bond to see how successful it has been over a period of time. This information can aid in your decision-making about which avenues you want to use to invest your money, with those avenues that yield the greatest return naturally rising to the top of your list. The point of the investment is not about the amount of money you put in; it's about the opportunity you have to make an even greater return.

When God tells you to obey, He is asking you to make an investment. He is asking you to give everything you have with the promise of receiving even more in return. The investment God wants us to make is far greater than any earthly investment. While earthly investments come with a risk of loss, God has a flawless track record from eternity past for always rewarding His people with far more than they deserve.

We live in a culture that celebrates the pleasures of sin while minimizing the consequences of it. Our culture scoffs at a life lived in obedience to God, making it seem as if there's no point to such efforts.

Dear friend, do not buy into the lies of the enemy. God will see to it that you are rewarded for your investment of obedience to Him.

Paul reminded us of this concept when he said, "And let us not grow weary of doing good, for in due season we will reap, if we do not give up" (Galatians 6:9). The writer of Hebrews also speaks of the rewards we'll receive for living an obedient life: "And without faith it is impossible to please him, for whoever would draw near to God must believe that he exists

> " God will see to it that you are rewarded for your investment of obedience to Him. "

and that he rewards those who seek him" (Hebrews 11:6).

Don't read past that too fast. This verse says that those who draw near to God—those who have a sense of vibrancy in their spiritual life—have an understanding of the fact that God rewards those who seek Him. They have faith to know that their efforts are not futile. They have the assurance that their obedience is an investment in a future return that is bigger, better, and far greater than their current reality.

Furthermore, drawing near is a privilege not afforded to everyone. The ability to approach God in personal relationship is something given freely only to those who accept the blood of Christ to cover their sins and invite Jesus to be Lord of their life. It is a blood-bought privilege that we so often take for granted, settling instead for behaving as mere acquaintances with God, looking on from a comfortable distance.

You will reap and you will be rewarded if you just stay the course. Finish strong. As uncomfortable as it might be, resolve to destroy whatever God brings to your attention and commit to the process of Christ-likeness that God has started in you.

No Shortcuts

Have you ever noticed that sometimes it seems easier to read books about the Bible rather than the Bible itself?

At times, it's enticing to look for a shortcut or a magic pill in our walk with God. We'd rather have someone tell us what we need to do to get closer to God rather than figuring it out with God ourselves. It's like we're looking for step-by-step instructions that we can latch onto and replicate in the hope that we can have the same encounter someone else experienced. In the awesome workbook *Experiencing God*, Henry Blackaby and Claude King quip that if Moses had authored a book called *My Burning Bush Experience*, crowds by the thousands would have flocked to nearby mountaintops in search of a burning bush all their own.[1]

Instead of looking to copy someone else's experience, we must learn to mine the Word of God and adopt a lifestyle of prayer and meditation before the Lord for ourselves. I thank God for those among us He's gifted to teach and explain His Word to His people, but I've come to discover that I can't foster an intimate, on-fire relationship with Jesus with secondhand knowledge alone. I have to get in there and discover some things for myself. I have to train my ear to His voice. Preachers and teachers can certainly assist me on my journey, but no one can do it for me.

It's funny how we say we want an intimate relationship with God but we shy away from the things that would make it so. We want rules, parameters, and guidelines rather than relationship.

One thing I know about relationships is that everyone's is different. After twelve years of marriage, it's become clear to me that no two marriages are the same because no two people are the same. Everyone's preferences and tastes are different. Over the years, I've wasted a lot of time looking at what I thought I knew of someone else's marriage relationship and trying to replicate it in my own. But that's not how relationships work. Principles can translate, such as open, honest communication, but how those principles are applied may vary from person to person.

Here's my encouragement to you: dare to travel the murky waters of developing your own unique, personal interaction with Jesus. You might have a friend who likes to journal. Great. Or maybe your Bible-study leader likes to sing hymns to the Lord. Wonderful. Some lady at church mentioned something about sitting in a dark room for hours on end. More power to her. But what do you and Jesus like to do together? How do you feel most connected to your Father? And if you don't know, then that's a wonderful place to start. Carve out some time with Him and try some things. Some of it will be uncomfortable. Some might make you feel silly. But don't give up. God rewards those who earnestly seek Him, so keep at it! Don't settle for a cookie-cutter interaction with Jesus you've heard about secondhand. Make it your own because it *is* your own. And He is your own.

God wants to have a unique relationship with you based on the personality, quirks, and disposition He breathed and wove into you. He knows how to speak so that you can understand—if you're willing to listen. And asking Him what in your life needs to be destroyed, transformed, and rebuilt is a beautiful gesture to show how much you want to know what He's got to say.

If you don't believe it, try Him. Test Him in it and watch Him work.

SPARK NOTES

Part 2
PURIFY

CHAPTER 6

TURNING UP THE HEAT

As a new mother more than ten years ago, I was a bit daunted by the task of keeping my child away from anything that could make her sick. I was big on shielding her from any germs, bugs, or nasty things that could cause illness. Ten years later, not much has changed. I'm still big into using hand sanitizer and coughing and sneezing into the fold of your arm rather than the same hand you're going to use to touch every kind of thing.

Lucky for me, I learned that it was actually very easy to cleanse and sanitize my new baby's pacifiers and bottles and things. All I needed to do was expose them to heat. A few minutes in a pot of boiling water was enough to rid these items of their impurities and return them to a safe state where they could be used again.

In your life and in my life, from time to time God will turn up the heat to remove impurities. It's in these moments that we have a critical decision to make. We can allow these situations to draw us closer to Jesus and stir up a deep devotion to Him, or we can allow these circumstances to draw us away from the Lord with feelings of doubt, fear, anger, and anxiety about why He would allow these things to happen.

In my own life, it seems like the times when I've felt the closest to God *and* the furthest from God have often included some sort of test, trial, or difficulty.

When disaster strikes, people who have allowed the Lord to ignite a passion for Him in their hearts consistently choose to rekindle their relationship with God and not regress in it.

The trials of life will either rekindle our relationship with Jesus or cause us to regress in our relationship with Jesus. The choice is yours.

The heat of fire has a way of bringing to the surface what was inside of a thing all along. In a similar way, God will present you with challenging circumstances to cause anything in you that's not like Him to bubble up to the surface and be made known so that He can drain it off and remove it from you.

> The trials of life will either rekindle our relationship with Jesus or cause us to regress in our relationship with Jesus. The choice is yours.

The early church faced every manner of trial and difficulty. Time after time, their very lives hung in the balance for the bold stand they made for the gospel of Christ. But coupled with the disciples' struggles and hardships is a beautiful truth we must remember: at just the right time, God will intervene to rescue and protect His own. Having full confidence in God's character, these early Christians allowed their difficulties to draw them that much closer to Jesus.

For example, after being beaten and charged not to speak in the name of Jesus by the Sanhedrin, the disciples left, "rejoicing that they were counted worthy to suffer dishonor for the name" (Acts 5:41). In Acts 13, the Jews incited persecution against the disciples, who were driven out of their district. But the disciples "shook off the dust from their feet against them and went to Iconium. And the disciples were filled with joy and with the Holy Spirit" (Acts 13:51–52).

For the early church, as the persecution and intensity of the fiery trials increased, so too did their zeal and passion for Jesus. In Acts 16, after Paul and Silas had been beaten and thrown into prison, they prayed and sang hymns to God (see verse 25). Their suffering actually awakened a desire to praise the Lord.

The Refining Fire

Purifying precious metals with fire is one of the oldest methods for refining them. In ancient days, a craftsman would sit next to a hot fire while the molten gold was stirred and skimmed to remove the impurities, or dross, that rose to the top due to the high temperatures.

As you are being tried in the fire, the loving Craftsman is right there, and His name is Jesus. He's not far off. He allows only that which will remove what He wishes to remove for the desired result.

A Matter of Perspective

The early believers viewed their sufferings with joy. Paul summarized their outlook in Philippians 3:10: "I may know him and the power of his resurrection, and may share his sufferings, becoming like him in his death."

It all sounds so good on paper. "When the stormy tempests roar, trust in Jesus!" But when it's your child who's been diagnosed with a terminal illness or your spouse who's been caught in the affair or your bank account that's always in the red, the way suddenly seems very unclear. When you find yourself in that place, here are some things you should remember:

Strength in Numbers

The early church made a habit of doing a lot of things—most things, in fact—together. They banded together as a community to support one another and tend to one another's needs. They worshiped together. They prayed together. They ate together. Acts 2:44 summarizes it simply: they "were together." In our modern-day culture, with its Internet churches, advanced technology, and virtual meet-ups, we've lost sight of the value of personal interaction. Technological advances offer many worthwhile benefits, but they can also make it easier for us to play right into the enemy's hand by retreating and isolating ourselves when we're being tested so that he can further discourage us.

Listen to me carefully. If you are going through a trying time right now in your faith and you are going it alone, you're making yourself an easy target for the enemy. If you stopped going to church, Bible study, prayer meeting, or whatever it is that you used to do to feed yourself spiritually that involved other people, then you run the risk of going backward in your walk with God and getting caught up in sin or some form of frivolous foolishness. Instead, find and connect with people you trust who will help stoke the embers of faith in your heart.

When my oldest daughter, Gabrielle, was just four months old, I noticed that she was beginning to lose her hair in a way that seemed unusual for a baby her age. We took her to see a dermatologist, where she was diagnosed with alopecia areata, which means "bald in spots." They told me that this was an autoimmune condition that causes her to spontaneously lose her hair. They encouraged me to stay positive but said it would likely affect her for the rest of her life.

As a new mother, I remember being so profoundly devastated. I researched the condition online, which certainly didn't help me feel any better. I was fixated on it, spending any spare moment examining her scalp in fear that new bald patches would appear. I even went so far as to buy a magnifying glass so that I could see every detail up close.

I was gripped with fear and anxiety. I remember lying in bed, unable to sleep, wondering how this whole thing was going to play out. I had thoughts of her going completely bald, and I wondered how I would deal with that. I contemplated her getting older and reaching milestones, such as prom and college and other important moments, and I wondered how we would deal with this issue.

Maybe you've never had a child struggle with alopecia, but I bet at one time or another you've come face to face with an extremely challenging situation, something you just didn't know how you were going to get through. You may be in one of those situations at this very moment. Well, here's my question to you: what are you going to do about it? Are you going to let it rekindle your relationship with God, or will you allow it to cause you to regress and stumble?

By God's grace, as I was going through the situation with my daughter's hair, I felt God pull me back to Him so tightly. At times, I was in such despair that all I could do was call on the name of the Lord. I remember going to work and being unable to focus because my mind and heart were so overcome with fear. So each day at my desk, I would open up a Word document and type out prayers, pouring out my heart and my anxiety before the Lord. I began to study my Bible even more.

But by far the one thing that helped me most was finding people I could be together with—people who were willing to walk through this situation with me, encourage me, and pray for me; people who I could call and just be honest with and say, "Hey, I'm really struggling right now," and they would offer prayer and a word of encouragement. Without this tribe, I just don't know how I would have made it. They helped me get my thoughts in line with the Word of God. When I started getting ahead of myself, worrying about ten and twenty years in the future, they reminded me to keep my eyes on the goodness and sufficiency of God in the present. When I was weak, they gave me strength. When I was anxious, they reminded me of the peace of God I had access to all the time. When I felt powerless, they led me to the all-powerful One.

In that situation, I felt very clearly in my heart from the very beginning that God would restore my daughter's hair. I had doubts along the way, but I still sensed it in my heart. It seemed that God confirmed it throughout the process, with so many people telling me definitively and emphatically that her condition would improve.

I remember sitting on the side of my bed one Saturday morning and looking at little Gabrielle and wondering, *If God has the ability to fix her condition, what in the world is He waiting on?* At that very moment, the story of the death of Lazarus was suddenly impressed upon my heart. John 11 tells us that Jesus got word that His good friend Lazarus was ill. Instead of running to Lazarus's bedside, Jesus waited. And waited. And waited. Even though He loved Lazarus (see John 11:5), by the time He got to Lazarus, he had already died. In fact, he'd been buried for four days. When Jesus finally arrived, He was greeted by quite a scene. Lazarus's sisters were mourning the death of their brother, and many of the Jews had come to comfort them. Lazarus's sister Mary fell at Jesus' feet, weeping for the death of her brother. The Jews were also weeping. Jesus, being so moved by the emotional scene before Him, began to weep Himself.

Jesus wept.

Jesus, who had already announced before He and His disciples started their trip that He was going to "awaken" Lazarus (John 11:11) and resuscitate him from the dead, was now weeping.

Am I the only one wondering what He had to be sad about?

The beauty of walking with Jesus through the trials of life we experience is that although He knows we will experience ultimate joy and restoration in eternity, He still weeps with us in our sorrow and shares in our pain in a very deep and profound way.

But why? Why would Jesus put Himself, Mary, Martha, Lazarus, and all the Jews gathered there in such a terrible and emotionally taxing situation? Why does He allow you and me to experience really uncomfortable, unimaginable, gut-wrenching things when He has the power to stop them at any time?

His Glory

I think this John 11 passage gives us two excellent reasons why God allows the fiery trials of life to purify us. The first is found in verse 4, when Jesus heard about Lazarus's illness. He said, "This illness does not lead to death. It is for the glory

of God, so that the Son of God may be glorified through it."
While God is keenly aware of our feelings and emotions and
how difficult many things in life are for us, He places a much
higher priority on His glory—the essence of who He is being
made known and people seeing Him in a deeper, more majestic
way. Above all else, He is concerned about people getting a
clearer view of the beauty, majesty, and power that is our great
God. At times, that can't happen when all of life's circumstances
are ideal. He will use bumps in the road to shine the spotlight
on Himself.

Your Belief

A second reason why God allows the fiery storms of life to
purify us is related to the first and is found sprinkled throughout
the passage by repetition of the word "believe." Before going to
see Lazarus, Jesus explained to the disciples that He was going
to raise Lazarus from the dead. He added, "For your sake I
am glad that I was not there, so that you may believe" (John
11:14). Jesus said that even though heartache was involved and
tears were shed, He was actually glad because if it got them to
believe, if it got them to a greater understanding and deeper
revelation about who He really is, then it was all worth it.

That's a pretty hard teaching. But I think it gives us insight
into the heart of God. God places an extremely high priority
on our not only knowing Him but also believing Him. We see
this idea further emphasized when Jesus arrived and said to
Martha, "I am the resurrection and the life. Whoever believes
in me, though he die, yet shall he live, and everyone who lives
and believes in me shall never die. Do you believe this?" (John
11:25).

Everything God allows us to experience has a higher
purpose: to solidify and grow our belief system. When we

experience something painful or unpleasant, God wants to use that to strengthen our faith to see that He is good, trustworthy, and faithful.

Above the specifics of the particular situation, God uses everything we experience to cause us to expand beyond textbook faith to a tried and true confidence in Him, even if we don't understand or agree with everything as it

> "God places an extremely high priority on our not only knowing Him but also believing Him."

unfolds. And dear Martha, in the midst of mourning and deep suffering, illustrated this principle in her faith-filled response to Jesus. She simply said, "Yes, Lord; I believe that you are the Christ, the Son of God, who is coming into the world" (John 11:27).

We need to learn a few things from Martha. First, notice that Martha's affirmation of her belief in Jesus in verse 27 didn't come at the end of the story, when Jesus resuscitated Lazarus back to life and joy had been restored. Her "Yes, Lord" came in the midst of pain, heartbreak, and anguish. It came in the midst of sorrow and perhaps even some frustration about Jesus' inopportune timing. But nonetheless, when prompted by the Savior to affirm her belief in His identity and power, her response was "Yes, Lord."

So what about you? As the storms continue to rage in your life and fiery trial after fiery trial come knocking at your door, what have these things caused you to believe about Jesus? As He shows you His heart and true identity in the midst of your pain, have you responded with a "Yes, Lord"?

But that's not all. Martha's "Yes, Lord" is just a preface to her declaration of what she believes. When she said she believes Jesus is the Christ, "who is coming into the world," she was actually making reference to Jesus as Messiah and Savior, the one who is the fulfillment of the prophecies of the Old Testament (see Psalm 118:26). She was affirming that He is more than a good man. He is more than a nice teacher. He is one with God, sent into the world to save us from our sins. In spite of her circumstances, Martha was declaring a confidence in the identity of Jesus and His power, dominion, and glory as the Son of God.

What about you? Are you able to affirm the glory and power of God, His identity, and His intentions for good and not evil, even in the midst of your trial?

As Jesus prepared to perform this miracle of bringing a dead man back to life, He instructed that the stone be taken away from Lazarus's tomb. Martha spoke up and, in essence, said, "Jesus, I love my brother, Lazarus, but I don't necessarily want to smell Lazarus right now. Do you really think it's a good idea to roll away the stone? It's been four days. There's got to be an odor by now."

In Jesus' response, He masterfully summarized the purpose behind this whole ordeal: "Did I not tell you that if you believed you would see the glory of God?" (John 11:40).

Belief.

Glory.

God is using any means necessary to bolster your belief in Him because, as that happens, you will get to know God in a deeper, fuller, more accurate way. You will see His glory.

SPARK NOTES

_____
_____
_____
_____
_____
_____
_____
_____
_____
_____
_____
_____
_____
_____
_____
_____
_____
_____
_____
_____
_____
_____
_____
_____
_____

CHAPTER 7

A MORE MATURE FAITH

S o, as I sat there on the side of my bed that day, wondering what the end would be for this little baby and this diagnosis, I heard the Spirit of the Lord whisper in my ear, "I've delayed My response to maximize My glory."

In Lazarus's case, by the time Jesus made an appearance, the Bible says that many of the Jews were there (see John 11:19). Therefore, many of the Jews witnessed this miracle of Lazarus being raised from the dead and saw Jesus' divine power—likely many more than if Jesus had performed the same miracle immediately after Lazarus's death. In that moment, God reminded me that often an important aspect of our trials is how God can use them in other people's lives to encourage them and point them to deeper belief in Jesus. So, in my situation, I was reminded that God was not aloof and far off. He was carefully manipulating the variables so that maximum glory for Himself would be achieved. In the meantime, what He wanted for me was to believe—all throughout the process, not just at the end.

One of my friends told me to lay hands on Gabrielle every night and pray for her. About three months after Gabrielle's diagnosis, I was praying for her one night and happened to notice that there were buds of hair growing in all the areas that had been completely bald. And I praised the Lord! But that wasn't when I started praising the Lord. I started praising Him before it happened—not because of how the situation would or wouldn't turn out but because God had given me deeper and deeper revelation into who He is and had grown my belief and had glorified Himself all throughout the process. So it wasn't the beginning of praise. It was the continuation of it.

By God's grace and despite what was I told, Gabrielle's hair hasn't stopped growing since. Please know that my experiences shared here are descriptive, not prescriptive. I'm simply describing an experience I had with the Lord. It's not instructive for you to do specifically what I did, nor is it implied that you should expect the same outcome. The point of it all is that God purifies us through trials by growing our belief in Him so that He can get all the glory.

Hope that Doesn't Disappoint

I can hear what some of you are thinking: *Well, Kelly, that's great that your little situation with you and your daughter worked out how you planned, but what about my prayers that weren't answered the way I wanted? What about those who died, despite fervent prayers that they would live? What about the marriage that ended*

> God purifies us through trials by growing our belief in Him so that He can get all the glory.

although I asked God for otherwise? What about the wayward children who refuse to listen to wise counsel?

Life is full of complex circumstances that don't afford us the opportunity for a neat and tidy explanation. Our God's ways are so much higher than ours that from the vantage point of Earth, it sometimes seems as though He's letting everything spin out of control and isn't keeping His word. Well, if you've ever felt that way, let me offer you this:

> Therefore, since we have been justified by faith, we have peace with God through our Lord Jesus Christ. Through him we have also obtained access by faith into this grace in which we stand, and we rejoice in hope of the glory of God. Not only that, but we rejoice in our sufferings, knowing that suffering produces endurance, and endurance produces character, and character produces hope, and hope does not put us to shame, because God's love has been poured into our hearts through the Holy Spirit who has been given to us. (Romans 5:1–3)

It seems rather odd that God would instruct us to rejoice in our sufferings. I rejoice when things are going well, when things are working in my favor, and when life is easy. But in this passage, Paul lays out the reason we can rejoice in suffering. And it's not because suffering is pleasant and makes us feel happy inside. Indeed, it does not. But suffering does do something far greater.

Suffering is a producer. It doesn't merely exist for its own benefit, but it brings about the existence of something else. This scripture teaches that suffering brings about endurance, or the ability to withstand hardships or great distress. But then it gets even better because endurance, too, is a producer. It produces proven character—it gives us a picture of what's truly been in us all along. But it doesn't stop there. Character is also a producer. It produces the best part: hope. So, according to these verses, the succession goes something like this:

Suffering → Endurance → Character → Hope

When this life is over and we see Jesus, we will not be put to shame for putting our hope in God. We will see that our toiling for Him was all worth it. If we can trust Him for the next life, we can trust Him for this one, too.

So when it hurts to hope—when life seems to be too inconsistent with hope and you're tempted to regress and distance yourself from God—ask God to rekindle you anew and remind you that you have reasons to hope and that your hope is in the One who will not disappoint. Regardless of the outcome of any particular situation, your hope will result in eternal life.

And that's something to rejoice about. Your suffering, as painful as it has been or will be, is jumpstarting a process that will make you more like Jesus and will bring to fruition the fulfillment of the hope we have in Him. Here's the million-dollar question every believer must be willing to honestly ask themselves:

Which do I value more: my comfort or my Christ-likeness?

I mentioned that my husband, Luvirt, and I have been married for twelve years. We're at that point where the years are starting to add up, so twelve years sounds impressive beside the amount of time a newlywed couple has been married. But compared to my grandparents, who've been married more than sixty years, it doesn't look like much.

In any case, I'm learning a lot along the way. I'll tell you that the way we're in love in year twelve is not the way we were in love in year one. The challenges we've faced together, the growing pains and disagreements, and the joys and achievements we've had have shaped us into something new and different. Not better. Not worse. Just different.

There were times along the path when I didn't want different. I wanted what we had in the beginning, exactly the way we had it. I longed for it. I thought that season of life was the best there was and I desperately wanted to recapture it. Meanwhile, I was overlooking the beautiful, new love that was sprouting before my eyes.

So it is in our walk with God. While God Himself always stays the same, our relationship with Him is ever-growing and evolving as He molds us more and more into His image. The trials He uses to purify us change the relationship because they redefine us and how we relate to God. Either they draw us closer to Him and rekindle a new, more mature love, or we allow them to entice us to regress and retreat from God, keeping Him at a distance in our life for fear He'll bring even more challenging things our way. The choice is entirely yours.

Like it or not, your trials will change you. How you let them change you and your relationship to God is up to you.

Building Blocks

Many of the groups, organizations, and companies I've been part of have often required me to participate in some sort of team-building day. You know the drill. There's always a battery of activities designed to get you to work together, talk to people you don't normally talk to, or work with people in a way you typically don't, all to build up the team's interpersonal skills.

I believe God takes us through a similar process. But instead of team building, it's about character building. One of the ways God glorifies Himself through the fiery trials of life is by bringing our character in closer alignment with His. He uses trials to impart to us noble characteristics such as courage, perseverance, and integrity. These verses illustrate this fact:

> Count it all joy, my brothers, when you meet trials of various kinds, for you know that the testing of your faith produces steadfastness. And let steadfastness have its full effect, that you may be perfect and complete, lacking in nothing. (James 1:2–4)

> In this you rejoice, though now for a little while, if necessary, you have been grieved by various trials, so that the tested genuineness of your faith—more precious than gold that perishes though it is tested by fire—may be found to result in praise and glory and honor at the revelation of Jesus Christ.
> (1 Peter 1:6–7)

Though the road you're traveling may be difficult, trust that God is right there every step of the way, inviting you into a closer, captivating, more mature relationship with Him.

SPARK NOTES

Part 3
LIGHT

CHAPTER 8

DO YOU KNOW WHO YOU ARE?

You are the light of the world. A city set on a hill cannot be hidden. Nor do people light a lamp and put it under a basket, but on a stand, and it gives light to all in the house. In the same way, let your light shine before others, so that they may see your good works and give glory to your Father who is in heaven. (Matthew 5:14–16)

Among fire's many functions and purposes, its ability to provide light is one of the most notable. One flickering flame can light up an entire room. So, when Jesus says that we are the light of not just a room, a hallway, or a house but the entire world, He seems to point to the idea that our presence should permeate any venue we are in.

Lights are meant to be prominent, visible, and out on display. Otherwise, they can't serve their purpose. You, believer in Christ, are meant to be prominent, visible, and out on display.

As you let your light shine, your fire for the Lord within your heart will intensify. And the natural outpouring will be good works—not for your own glory, accolades, or recognition, but for God's, and His alone.

It's so important that we recognize the significance of God calling us light before we jump in trying to do good works. Light is not something we do. The good works are what we do. But the light? It's just who we are. It is our very identity.

Many times, we feel that good works will keep our fire burning strong for the Lord. They won't. We think that if we could just find out what God wants us to do, what ministry He wants us to serve in, or what soup kitchen to volunteer in, then that will be enough to keep the embers of our faith going strong.

But we're the light of the world because we're in Jesus. It's not something we work for. So we don't need good works to gain God's approval or to stay in His good graces. Good works are what the light of the world will naturally do. So our focus, then, is not as much on the good works as it is on embracing our identity as light.

As you continue to discover and explore your identity as light through connection with the Father, the good works, the direction, clarity, purpose, and impact you're looking for will follow.

That's why I'm glad we didn't start here. I'm glad we talked about the fact that to truly stay the course, we need to surrender to God, allowing Him to wreck our lives, so to speak, to align us with Him. Then we must purpose in our minds to hold fast to God no matter what storms life may bring us because we know He's working a bigger purpose of purifying our hearts in the process.

It is our intimate, continual connection with God that teaches us who He is and, in effect, who we are—our identity. This sets the stage to use our gifts, talents, and abilities to accomplish good works for the Lord. If we bypass the process, we run the risk of attempting to do good works but still feeling empty and unsatisfied because we haven't allowed God to fill us.

Our chief emphasis should not be on *doing*. It must be on *being*—being in relationship with the Father and being exactly what God called us to be: the light of the world.

You must first allow God to do an inner work in you so that, as Henry Blackaby and Claude King say, you will have the character to match the assignment.[1] Many times we beg for the big assignments but do not have the character to match. But if you first understand and embrace your identity as God's child, the light of the world, then something remarkable will emerge: your true authentic self, wholly submitted to God, devoid of all pretense.

Those who embrace their identity as light will find their soul's passion for Jesus intensified. What is the driving force behind these kinds of people? The Holy Spirit.

Follow the Leader

If anyone understood their identity as light, it was the early church. For these first believers, the Holy Spirit was the driving force behind each and every thing they did. These Christians did not consider following God's leading via the Holy Spirit an optional exercise, one alternative among many to be considered. The Spirit's leading was their lifeblood, their sustenance, and their heartbeat.

The Scriptures teach that the Holy Spirit is not an "it," nor is He a force. He is a person. He is the third person of the

Trinity, meaning that He is fully God, just as the Father and the Son are fully God. The Spirit can give commands (see Acts 1:2), is said to author Scripture (see Acts 1:16; 4:25; 28:25), has the ability to speak (see Acts 13:2–4), and gives direction (see Acts 28:25). If you haven't been able to tell already, the Holy Spirit is awesome!

During Jesus' earthly ministry, He foretold the coming of the Spirit. He said that this Spirit would be a Helper, or helping Presence, that would be with them forever. And not only would He be with them, but also He would be in them (see John 14:15–17). Jesus went on to tell His disciples, "It is to your advantage that I go away, for if I do not go away, the Helper will not come to you. But if I go, I will send him to you. . . . When the Spirit of truth comes, he will guide you into all the truth, for he will not speak on his own authority, but whatever he hears he will speak, and he will declare to you the things that are to come" (John 16:7, 13).

If you are a believer in Jesus Christ, then God lives in you through the person of the Holy Spirit, and He's not going anywhere. Paul highlighted the permanence of the Spirit's presence when he said, "In him you also, when you heard the word of truth, the gospel of your salvation, and believed in him, were sealed with the promised Holy Spirit" (Ephesians 1:13). Through the Holy Spirit, God protects and preserves us until we reach the fulfillment of our salvation in eternity with Jesus.

The early church was so impactful because they leaned wholeheartedly on the Holy Spirit to empower them to walk out their calling as the light of the world. These ideals played out in two ways:

1. Control

To yield to the Holy Spirit's leading and direction is to willingly give Him control of our lives. Ephesians 5:18 says, "Do not get drunk with wine, . . . but be filled with the Spirit." In other words, don't let alcohol control your mind, judgment, and decision making. Instead, let the Spirit be the One to take control.

As believers, we are indwelt by God's Spirit at the moment of salvation. But that doesn't necessarily mean that we've given Him control of every area of our lives. It doesn't necessarily mean that we live each day to please Him and carry out His commands. It doesn't even mean that we're willing to yield our plans to His. All those things are wrapped up in the command here to be filled with the Spirit, or to be controlled by the Spirit.

The salvation of our souls when we are indwelt with the Spirit is a one-time event. But the command to be filled with the Spirit is written in the present imperative in Greek, the original language of the New Testament. Present imperative is just a fancy way of saying that being filled with the Holy Spirit is not a singular event. It's ongoing. It's a choice and a lifestyle. Another way to say it would be "keep on being filled."

The first time I was introduced to this concept in any detail, I was in college. What stood out to me the most was that I had the chance to be controlled by the Spirit to help accomplish God's plans on the earth. I had an amazing opportunity in front of me, and I was opting out, favoring instead to do life on my own terms.

In the famous story of Pinocchio, a wooden puppet sets out on a quest to become a real boy. While it seems that life apart from the marionette strings would be the ideal situation, Pinocchio soon finds out that without the loving protection of the craftsman and his puppet strings, he gets into quite a bit of trouble.

Sometimes we're like that puppet and desire to just be free of the demands and dictates of the strings, when God calls all the shots. Little do we know that those strings provide loving protection and empower us for our life ahead.

The early church was a puppet of sorts, with the string master being the Holy Spirit. They "turned the world upside down" (Acts 17:6) by the Spirit of God and Him alone.

When we are empowered by the Holy Spirit, it will fuel the flames of our faith. It is our privilege to do so as the light of the world. But if we're not empowered, we won't be able to consistently live out the call of God on our life.

If you had to assign a percentage, between 0 percent and 100 percent, how much control does the Holy Spirit have over your life?

> " When we are empowered by the Holy Spirit, it will fuel the flames of our faith. "

This can be a difficult question to answer. Thankfully, Ephesians 5 gives us some help in determining how much control we've allowed the Holy Spirit to have. What follows the command in Ephesians 5 to be filled with the Spirit is a very practical picture of what a Spirit-filled life looks like:

- Praise to God (5:19)
- Thankfulness and gratitude (5:20)
- Submission to the authority and order established by God (5:21)

Paul took it even further within the family and work structure to illustrate the Spirit-filled life:

- Wives in submission to husbands, as to the Lord (5:22)
- Wives respect husbands (5:33)
- Husbands sacrificially love their wives (5:25–32)
- Children obey and honor their parents (6:1–2)
- Obey authority—government and employers (6:5)

Galatians 5:22–23 gives us further indicators of the level of which the Holy Spirit is controlling us. The fruit, or the byproduct, of the Spirit's work in our lives will be produced:

- Love
- Joy
- Peace
- Patience
- Kindness
- Goodness
- Faithfulness
- Gentleness
- Self-control

Do you see these characteristics displayed in an increasing way in your life? If the Spirit is in control, you will see high levels of the above attributes and characteristics in your life and a decreasing level of things that oppose these attributes. But did you notice what wasn't on the list? Saying big words while praying. Church attendance. Attending church for a long time. Being gifted or talented. Singing really well. Having lots of Bible knowledge.

So let's consider the question again: how much control does the Holy Spirit have over your life?

A big indicator is how you treat other people. If you are not loving, kind, gentle, or all the other indicators the Scripture gives us, then it's highly likely there's some room for improvement in the area of Holy Spirit filling.

If your percentage isn't as high as you'd like, then let me encourage you with what I learned many years ago on a college campus: it's yours for the taking.

Again, the early church gives us useful tips: "And they devoted themselves to the apostles' teaching and the fellowship, to the breaking of bread and the prayers" (Acts 2:42). This community of believers was so powerful because it depended upon the Holy Spirit. This verse gives us a glimpse into the activity that characterized this community. In turn, it gives us a glimpse into the Spirit-filled life. They . . .

1. devoted themselves to the Word of God
2. devoted themselves to fellowship, or one another, and prayed

If you're looking to grant access to the Holy Spirit to more of your life, then incorporating these three practices on a regular basis will keep you on the right path.

2. Power

Do you know one very practical reason why you should yield control to the Holy Spirit? Because you need His power. A yielded life gives you access to the Spirit's power. Because the New Testament believers yielded control to the Holy Spirit, they freely experienced the Spirit's power. Make no doubt about it, the Spirit of God is a Spirit of power. Jesus told the disciples, "You will receive power when the Holy Spirit has come upon you" (Acts 1:8). And it's also no shock that Peter declared that

"God anointed Jesus of Nazareth with the Holy Spirit and with power" (Acts 10:30).

This power certainly includes the miraculous, the showy, and the demonstrative, such as raising Lazarus from the dead or healing the sick. But it also includes returning a blessing for evil, as Stephen did. After boldly witnessing for Jesus and knowing his death was imminent via stoning, "he cried out in a loud voice, 'Lord, do not hold this sin against them'" (Acts 7:60). He was so reminiscent of Jesus, asking that His killers be forgiven because they didn't understand the magnitude of what they were doing. We can see a similar example when Paul and Silas were in jail. A great earthquake opened the prison doors and loosened everyone's shackles, but it was the power of the Spirit of God that held Paul and Silas back from running for freedom. Instead, they showed compassion and concern for the jailer and shared the gospel with him so that even his family could be saved (see Acts 16).

Time after time we see the Holy Spirit empowering the early believers to walk in such a high degree of boldness and faith that it seems foreign to us. The cowering in doubt and fear that the modern church is often crippled by seems foreign to this band of believers. Yet the same Spirit they walked in, we have access to as well.

As we yield control to the Spirit, we will manifest His power, which shines as a light in darkness and makes our identity as witnesses for Jesus all the clearer.

> We won't walk in our full identity until we walk in the Holy Spirit.

We won't walk in our full identity until we walk in the Holy Spirit.

SPARK NOTES

CHAPTER 9

MARCHING ORDERS

We established in the previous chapter that Jesus said that we are the light of the world and that through our good works, the whole world will be able to give Him glory. To fully complete those good works, we have to embrace our identity as light, which means we have to depend on the Spirit. I want to give you three characteristics of Spirit-filled people who embrace their identity as light.

1. Boldness

We've already pointed out that lights are prominent, visible, and out on display. You know another way to say that? Lights are bold. By design, lights are vivid, clear, and strong. They don't cower in the presence of darkness. No way. Just their mere presence changes the whole atmosphere around them.

If you want your passion for God to heighten, then you can't be afraid to be bold. Time and time again, we see the early believers praying for and being known for their boldness (see Acts 4:13, 29). Boldness here means "Spirit-inspired courage and confidence to speak in spite of any danger or threat."[1] For these early believers and for present-day believers in many parts of the

> If you want your passion for God to heighten, then you can't be afraid to be bold.

world, a bold, adamant witness for faith in Jesus could mean the end of their lives. But through the empowering Spirit, they stand firm.

This is a problem for some of us. We'd much rather live a quiet, secret faith that no one needs to know about. We live our lives all but hiding our faith and wonder why our flame is fizzling out. We'd much rather blend in with the crowd.

But you can't blend in and be light. You can't blend in and keep up a passion and fervor for God that stands the test of time. You can't fly under the radar and have God ignite a hunger for Him within you. You have to choose one or the other.

What if people don't like us or ostracize us for our beliefs? we think. *What if people don't agree with us and distance themselves from us because of it?*

To these objections, I have but one question: Do you want to be light or do you want to be liked?

You have to decide right now whether you want praise from God or praise from people. Which one is it going to be? You can't have both. Praise from people offers the short-term allure of acceptance and approval. At the same time, if you yearn for those things more than you seek to please Jesus, then your divided heart will squelch the flames of your passion for Him. That's why Paul said, "For am I now seeking the approval of man, or of God? Or am I trying to please man? If I were still trying to please man, I would not be a servant of Christ" (Galatians 1:10).

"What if I fall short and mess up?" we think. *"Isn't it better if I keep my faith quiet just in case so that I don't appear hypocritical?"*

My dear, do you trust the power of God to keep you or not? Does the Spirit who raised Christ from the dead live in you or not? God isn't asking for perfection. There is only one perfect One, and His name is Jesus. All God wants you to do is have a genuine yielding of control and a commitment to Him to do His will.

Pastor and teacher Tony Evans likens the Christian walk to Scrubbing Bubbles, the bathroom cleaner with the tagline "We work hard so you don't have to."[2] God has given you His Holy Spirit to do the heavy lifting in your Christian life. All you have to do is stop objecting, get over your fear, and yield.

When my family and I moved into our current home ten years ago, one of the new features I noticed that our old home didn't have was dimmer switches on many of the light panels, which allowed us to control how bright the light would shine. My kids thought it was fun to play with the controls to see what kind of effect the different degrees of brightness would have.

I wonder if some of us have put the dimmer switch onto our Christianity. In some settings, we push the switch of our faith all the way up, shining as brightly as can be. But in other settings, to avoid offending anyone, our faith seems to fade to dark.

The Spirit-filled life is not one of constant tweaking and adjusting, where our faith is only evident in certain situations or settings. It is a life of boldness, a complete, consistent commitment to Christ no matter where we are.

Does boldness mean being overtly and purposefully obnoxious, terrorizing anyone who dares to stand in your path with an opposing viewpoint? No. Whatever you do, do it in love. "If possible, so far as it depends on you, live peaceably with all" (Romans 12:18). Boldness simply means speaking up and not backing down, even if the consequences are undesirable.

The early church prayed for boldness (see Acts 4:29). I believe much of what they accomplished was in answer to their prayers. In what areas do you need to pray for more boldness?

2. Patient Persuasion

Pockets of the Christian community have gotten a bad reputation for hitting people over the head with the Word of God in an attempt to bring them to an understanding of the truth. Their rude, mean-spirited technique has done little to draw people to the God they preach about. I think these pockets develop because we forget our identity as light. Light does not walk up to darkness and tell it to stop being dark. It does not have to be mean and disrespectful, screaming to let darkness know that it means business. You know all light has to do to have an impact? Be present. Be prominent. Be visible. Be out on display.

Paul gave us an example to follow in Acts 19:8: "And he entered the synagogue and for three months spoke boldly, reasoning and persuading them about the kingdom of God." The "reasoning" referred to speaks to the idea of patient persuasion and relationship building over time rather than an angry, one-sided sermon. How many times, when we've encountered someone who held a view different from our faith system, did we see them as an argument to win, a bother or a roadblock rather than a real person who needs real salvation?

We must couple our passion for truth with compassion and understanding.

Acts 17:16 says, "Now Paul was waiting for them at Athens, his spirit was provoked within him as he saw that the city was full of idols." "Spirit" in this verse doesn't refer to the Holy Spirit. It refers to Paul's human spirit. It means he was really troubled to see that this city worshiped false gods. But check out what Paul did in response: "So he reasoned in the synagogue with the Jews and the devout persons, and in the marketplace every day with those who happened to be there." He didn't spew anger or hate. He reasoned. He patiently persuaded. And not just one time. It was his habit to do this every day. His heart for the people is so reminiscent of Jesus in Matthew 9:

> And Jesus went throughout all the cities and villages, teaching in their synagogues and proclaiming the gospel of the kingdom and healing every disease and every affliction. When he saw the crowds, he had compassion for them, because they were harassed and helpless, like sheep without a shepherd. (Matthew 9:35–36)

The crowd represents those who don't yet believe, those who need patient persuasion. When Jesus saw the crowd, He had compassion. He saw much deeper than what could be perceived with the naked eye. He saw their true spiritual condition. He saw them with no spiritual guidance, vulnerable, without protection, unable to help themselves. That's why, as the scripture says, He called them "harassed and helpless, like sheep without a shepherd."

When you look at the crowds, what do you see? Do you see an inconvenience? A nuisance? Another exhausting project?

When you see the crowd, what do you feel? Superior? Aggravated? Brokenhearted?

When you see the crowd, what do you do? Do you help? Turn a blind eye? Condemn?

If feelings of arrogance and superiority overtake you as you survey the crowd, it's snuffing out your fire for Jesus.

Whom do you need to patiently persuade? Toward whom do you need to show compassion?

3. Unity

One of the ways believers will live out their identity as light, and signal to a lost world the deity of Christ, is through their unity with one

> Toward whom do you need to show compassion?

another. This is what Jesus prayed for the believers: "that they may all be one, just as you, Father, are in me, and I in you, that they also may be in us, so that the world may believe that you have sent me" (John 17:21).

> Believers live out their identity as light through their unity with one another.

The early church understood this idea. They were "of one heart and soul, and no one said that any of the things that belonged to him was his own, but they had everything in common" (Acts 4:32). Today's modern landscape is much different. We live in a "me and Jesus" society, yet when God saved us, He grafted us into a "we and Jesus" movement. He planted us into a collective body that He will use to change the world.

After Peter's confession of faith in Matthew 16, Jesus pointed ahead to a time in the future, a time that includes the era in which you and I are now living. It is a time when His followers will be known as the church, or *ekklesia* in Greek.

> And I tell you, you are Peter, and on this rock I will build my church, and the gates of hell shall not prevail against it. I will give you the keys of the kingdom of heaven, and whatever you bind on earth shall be bound in heaven, and whatever you loose on earth shall be loosed in heaven. (Matthew 16:18–19)

The church is the community of all true believers for all time. This unique community called the church belongs to Christ Himself. The church is the mechanism by which God will make His kingdom, or supreme rule, known throughout the earth. Matthew 24:14 says, "And this gospel of the kingdom will be proclaimed throughout the whole world as a testimony to all nations, and then the end will come." The means by which God will carry His message to the nations is through His church. Within the church, God is assembling the "called-out ones" (or *ekklesia*) to legislate change in each and every sector of society. If you are a believer in Jesus Christ, then this means you!

As members of the church, you and I have a weighty task ahead of us, but Jesus says our success on this mission is sure. In Matthew 16:18, "a city's gates" represent the city's defenses, power, and security. So when Jesus says that the gates of hell will not prevail against the church, He assures us that the defenses of the kingdom of darkness will never, ever overpower the church.

Don't miss that.

No matter how many gut-wrenching blows the church takes to its head and its heart, it will prevail. There is no stopping the move of God. Not even the gates of hell thwart God's plans and purposes.

Jesus also gives insight into what He expects the church to do. He has given the church some keys—and not just any old keys. These are keys to the Kingdom (see Matthew 16:20). The idea of giving keys indicates the fact that Jesus has given the church authority—entrance to the Kingdom through belief in the gospel.

But how can the church legislate change, how can the church serve as "called-out ones," if, by all outward appearances, we appear to be no different than anyone else?

How can we be unified when we are jealous and envious of one another, motivated by our own selfish pride, not wanting to see others do better than we are? How can the church have the unity Jesus prayed for if we are judgmental and legalistic, shouting loudly at our brothers and sisters where the Word of God remains quiet? How can our light shine when we snuff it out with sloppy, immoral living and mistreatment of one another?

All too often, we apply the code of the streets to the church and wonder why our soul's passion for God is on life support. People of God, we cannot dismiss the unity mandated in Scripture as a polite suggestion that can be given or taken. Could it be that the lack of fire for Jesus in our individual lives is due in part to how we've abandoned the importance of the corporate unity of the body of Christ?

The Word of God calls believers a body. Does your body not need to be in one accord to function properly? If a part of your body becomes infected with agents that aren't on board with the main agenda of the body and don't want to come under submission to that main agenda, then it's called cancer. It's a disease, and it adversely affects every other area of the body. We're called to work together. And we can't do that if we lack unity.

This isn't about liking everyone. This is about placing a higher priority on our mandate to be the light of the world, the world's visual representation of the kingdom of God, than on our personal preferences and comfort.

As I write this, a situation or two come to mind where I have to honestly ask myself some questions. Am I behaving in this situation to put emphasis on peace and unity, or are my feelings and personal hang-ups running the show? If I'm not willing to make the necessary changes to my behavior, then am I okay with the inevitable negative effect it will have on my personal passion and fervor for the Lord?

People of God, we are the light of the world. We are called to be a bold, patiently persuading, unified people who do everything for the sole purpose of showing off the unparalleled goodness of our God. When we walk in this identity, the flames of our fire for Jesus will shine bright.

SPARK NOTES

CONCLUSION

Well, it looks like we have reached the end of our journey. We traveled the stormy waters of letting God disarm and destroy anything and everything in our life that's not pleasing to Him. We walked through the desert place of difficulty, where God purifies us, beckoning us to come closer and not move away. We arrived as the light of the world, poised and ready to embrace our true identity and walk into boldness, patient persuasion, and unity. And with each step, the fire grew. The intensity increased. And we knew that something had been ignited in us that the world could never take away: a genuine desire to please Jesus out of a humbled, surrendered heart.

Too often we are satisfied with an uninspiring walk with God, filled with robotic activities, rote rituals, and strict rules, an interaction devoid of any fire or true passion. God wants more for you. I hope you now see that a spiritual walk of fire, excitement, passion, and—dare I say—enjoyment are well within your reach. We won't have a life free of troubles and concerns this side of eternity. But God created you and me to know Him, enjoy Him, and interact with Him in a way that gives us purpose, direction, and fulfillment.

What Next?

Here is my challenge to you. God forbid these words remain hidden within the pages of this book and are not used by the Holy Spirit as an agent of change in your life. Far be it that this book has been empty theoretical rhetoric that never intersects with your daily experience. So I challenge you to take some time away. It might even be five minutes locked in the bathroom away from a demanding job, a hungry husband, or needy little ones. But I challenge you to get before God to reflect and ask Him to pinpoint what He wants you to do because of what you've read.

For some of you, He probably already impressed some things upon your heart as you've been reading. Don't dismiss that! That was the Holy Spirit speaking to you, tugging at your heart to align your life more closely with His will and His Word. That was the Holy Spirit, awakening within you an awareness of how to be drawn closer to Him and what He wants you to do. That was the Holy Spirit, doing the work that He delights to do: to ignite.

So go forward. Run to God, never from Him. The hills may be steep, but He will strengthen you for the journey. And as you step forward, you will see that your heart has been set ablaze for the things of God.

Through His Son, God has given us access to everything we need to consistently live a life of vigor, boldness, and passion for Him that will change not only our lives but also the world—if only we would grab hold of it. May we live our lives laser-focused on that mission.

Now, go be great.

SPARK NOTES

NOTES

Chapter 4 – Counting Wrong
1. John MacArthur, "Men Who Turned the World Upside Down, Part 1" (sermon, Grace Community Church, Sun Valley, CA, October 21, 1973).
2. David Kinnaman and Gabe Lyons, *unChristian: What a New Generation Really Thinks About Christianity . . . and Why It Matters* (Grand Rapids, MI: Baker Books, 2007), 15, 48.

Chapter 5 – Well Worth the Effort
1. Henry T. Blackaby and Claude V. King, *Experiencing God: Knowing and Doing the Will of God* (Nashville, TN: Lifeway Press, 1990), 73.

Chapter 8 – Do You Know Who You Are?
1. Henry T. Blackaby and Claude V. King, *Experiencing God: Knowing and Doing the Will of God* (Nashville, TN: Lifeway Press, 1990), 39.

Chapter 9 – Marching Orders
1. *ESV Study Bible* (Wheaton, IL: Crossway, 2008), 2,088.
2. Tony Evans, *The Fire That Ignites: Living in the Power of the Holy Spirit* (Sisters, OR: Multnomah, 2003), 70.

Let's connect! Stay in the know with Kelly and tell us what you think about *Ignite!* Continue the conversation using **#delighttoignite**.

@whenthegalsgather

@whenthegalsgather

@galsgather

When the Gals Gather

www.whenthegalsgather.com

CPSIA information can be obtained
at www.ICGtesting.com
Printed in the USA
FFOW02n1939200418
46300194-47832FF